Don't be a
Corporate Chintu

**Unlock your potential to break
the Corporate Politics**

The phrase "Don't Be a Corporate Chintu" or "Don't Be a Corporate Fool" is essentially an admonition to avoid being naive, gullible, or easily manipulated in a corporate or business environment.

This book will protect you from corporate politics trap and help to make informed decisions to avoid common pitfalls, including being seen as inexperienced or foolish. This book provides a comprehensive understanding of corporate culture, strategies, and related concepts. It is designed for individuals at various levels of corporate hierarchy, including aspiring professionals, those new to the corporate world, those currently working in corporate culture, entrepreneurs, middle management, top management, and owners of established companies.

The book offers clear and professional insights into the complexities of corporate life, equipping readers with the knowledge and tools needed to succeed in their professional careers.

Corporate Chintu

Author: Pankaj Chandan

Author: Pankaj Chandan

ABOUT THE AUTHOR

Pankaj Chandan is an accomplished author and an expert in the field of Human Resource and Administration. With over two decades of experience in managing a diverse range of Human Resource and Admin functions.

Over the course of his career, Pankaj has worked with several multinational corporations, leading the Human Resource and administration functions of the companies. He has developed expertise in talent management, employee engagement, performance management, and leadership development.

Pankaj's book, Don't be a "Corporate Chintu", is a reflection of his extensive experience and expertise.

The book offers practical insights and strategies for managing a successful career in the corporate world, covering topics that someone can relate with.

Pankaj serves as a mentor and coach to up-and-coming professionals, offering them valuable guidance and support as they work towards achieving their goals and realizing their potential.

<u>Link up with the Wordsmith: Join forces with the Brain</u>

Author: Pankaj Chandan

CONTENTS

Author: Pankaj Chandan

TAPPING INTO

UNCHARTED TERRITORY

"**Corporate Politics**" is the complex set of relationships, behaviours, and power dynamics that exist among individuals in a corporate or organizational setting. It involves the pursuit of individual interests and agendas, which may or may not be in line with the organization's overall goals and objectives. Corporate politics often involve the use of informal networks, alliances, and other tactics to gain power and influence.

It has a significant impact on strategic decisions and it is important for organizations to be aware of this. By understanding and managing the power dynamics within the organization, leaders should ensure that their decisions are based on the best interests of the company.

Race of Power: In any organization, power hungry people can be a huge detriment to progress. These people often use their power and try to push their own agendas, make decisions without proper consultation, and manipulate others to get what they want. This type of behaviour can lead to a culture of mistrust and a lack of respect for colleagues. It can also impede progress and stifle creativity.

The first step to dealing with power hungry people is to recognize the signs. These people tend to be overly aggressive, controlling, and self-promoting. They may also be quick to blame others for their own mistakes and always want to be in charge. It is important to keep an eye out for these behaviours and to address them as soon as they arise.

Once these behaviour have been identified, it is important to address them head-on. Encourage open communication and collaboration among team members and make sure that everyone has a chance to voice their opinions. This will help ensure that all perspectives are considered before making decisions.

You should also set clear boundaries and expectations for everyone in the organization. Power hungry people often take advantage of unclear expectations to push their own agenda. Make sure everyone understands what their roles and responsibilities are and that their behaviour is held to a certain standard.

Finally, empower other team members to make decisions and take initiative. This will help prevent power hungry people from feeling like they need to take control of every decision. It will also create a more collaborative and productive environment.

Power hungry people can be detrimental to any organization. By recognizing the signs and addressing them head-on, you can help create an environment of trust and respect and ensure that everyone has a chance to contribute.

Informal Groups: Organisations often have informal groups that can influence politics within the company. These groups are made up of employees who share a common interest or belief and work together to achieve their goals. Although informal groups are not formally organized, they can still have a significant impact on the organization's politics.

Informal groups can be formed around a variety of topics, such as the type of work, the type of people, or the type of technology used in the organization. For example, a group of young, tech-savvy employees may form an informal group to discuss the best ways to use technology in the workplace. This group could influence the company's politics by advocating for changes that would help the organization become more technologically advanced.

It can also be formed around shared values or beliefs. For example, a group of employees may come together to advocate for more workplace diversity. This could influence the organization's politics by pushing for changes in hiring practices or policies that promote diversity.

Informal groups shared sense of identity. For example, a group of female employees may come together to advocate for better representation of women in the workplace. This group could influence the company's politics by pushing for changes such as providing more resources for female employees or creating a more inclusive work environment.

It can also be formed to share desire for change. For example, a group of employees may come together to advocate for better pay and benefits. This group could influence the company's politics by pushing for changes in compensation and benefits packages.

Denouement: Informal groups can have a powerful influence on the politics of an organization. By advocating for change and working together to achieve their goals, these groups can push for reforms that can benefit the entire organization. It is important for organizations to be aware of the influence of informal groups and to take their interests into account when making decisions.

DHRITARASHTRA

Mr. Sharma; boss yelled in a strong voice while pointing him to come inside the meeting room.

Arvind Sharma yes, it is me who was called in the meeting room by my boss "Mr. Dutta" in front of all my colleagues in a very unappropriated manner.

With lot of confusion I peeped inside from the meeting room door. May I get in Sir? He nodded and asked me to sit.

It was a pin drop silence all around. I tried hard to recall what I had done wrong and I was struggling with the millions of thoughts bouncing on my head in a friction of the seconds.

Dutta 16 year's old employee who is famous for his inhuman and ruthless behaviour is the star in the eyes of the Management don't know for what reasons. He always tries to pretend that he is the only person who is running the organisation and surprisingly the Management is also thinking on the same tone.

"What the shit you had done?" - soul trembling sudden shout of Mr. Dutta dragged me from my thoughts seems like a little dog just crushed half of it by the heavy truck on the highway.

Whatt – Whatt Sir – I said it quietly. Being a new in the organisation with only couple of months experience one can't raise his/her voice, like he did. My conscious says common "Sharma" you are not a pity lamb tied with a rope and waiting for the butcher, who is busy sharping his cleaver to end your life.

He "Mr. Dutta" my so-called "Boss" pointed out the email, that I had sent to the client, where I had asked for the clarifications for the better understanding regarding the first-time order.

Before I could say anything regarding that email he again shouted – "Don't you have brains" why had you not consulted me before sending this type of email directly to the client? I was quite surprised that when client had no issues, then why he is creating such a scene.

I remember when I had a discussion with client couple of hours before regarding their first-time order and tried to understand their requirements, that time client had appreciated me for the courtesy call and my efforts, then suddenly what had happened wrong in the entire scenario. Where I am wrong man? Feeling of utter disappointment rushed to my nerves system. Even though I tried hard but my dismay turned to salted water drop, started rolling out from my eyes.

I recollect all my courage and asked – Where I was wrong Sir? This is the first time ever he had a rebut from someone.

The person who is giving lectures on cooperation, understanding, team spirit and empathy during my induction time, is now in front of me, losing his temper. First time I experienced the contradiction of "Words & Action" from a professional looking mouth.

Out of all one-and-a-half-hour monologue, yes it was a monologue because he was the only one who is putting his point forward and not in a mood to listen to the other side. Soon It was clear to me that interaction with the client directly made him furious and may put him on the back seat of the car doing nothing.

How one who is in the organisation from last 16 years for whatever reasons can digest the appreciation given by the client to the couple of month's old employee.

I can relate why working in his team is tough, why one never gets elevated, why everyone who is working under him are behaving like a slave and why these types of Bosses are getting hefty salaries and promotion every now and then.

I had heard once that "People leave Bosses not the Companies" and now I experienced it by my own.

Denouement: Top Management should spare some time out of their busy schedule to do some self-introspection that for running the business just numbers are not sufficient.

People who are working for them, giving their valuable time, energy and efforts to achieve the organisational goals are not machines without emotions and feelings.

Top Management should not behave like a "Dhritarashtra" who was bond by the love of his son "Duryodhana" end up with the destruction of the entire empire.

Manager's behaviour and treatment towards employees can have a significant impact on their motivation and well-being. In this story, Mr. Dutta's rude and unprofessional demeanour towards Mr. Sharma had a negative impact on him, causing him to feel demotivated and disheartened.

This highlights the importance of treating employees with respect and empathy.

Furthermore, it shows that top management should prioritize the well-being and happiness of employees rather than just focusing on the bottom line. A workplace that values and supports its employees is more likely to foster a positive and productive culture.

SERVICE REWARD

Today I got my "Service Reward" of continuous eleven years of best services in my company.

Super-One-Telelinks is India's leading telecom company where I was working for more than a decade and today was the reward day.

I always started my day with scrolling my inbox to plan the day ahead. As soon as I opened my computer an email popped up. It was from my manager.

Papa Papa, can you play with me? My 7 years old daughter Ritika came to me and requested me in her cute mesmerising voice. But I was busy in my office work so much that I forgot that it was 8:40pm and I had promised her that in evening we will go to the park for sure.

Can't you spend at least one day in entire week with us and for God's sake on "Sunday" at-least? my wife Preeti shouted on me from the kitchen.   She got fed up of my workaholic nature.

Ok yaar, please calm. You know what my profile is. I countered in return. But after all that was my problem, that my professional life started overpowering my personal life and I was not doing anything to improve this.

I closed my laptop and went to my daughter who is now upset sitting on the couch with a hope that Papa will come and play or take her to the park.

Preeti came and sat just near to me and said why are you spoiling your health? Why don't you talk to your manager? you are not a robot

Rishi to do all the work all alone. I nodded my head with an agreement.

The fact was that I had discussed this with my manager many times, but even though story was same. So, I decided to search for some good job options. With a continuous effort and so many job interviews I got selected in one of the premium companies but in different industry, who were offering me forty percent of the salary hike with other perquisites.

Preeti was very happy when I showed my Offer Letter to her. We celebrated that evening with a nice dinner at Barbeque that was near to our society.

Very next day I submitted my resignation without any discussion with my manager via an email, as one month's notice period was required to get the relieving letter and that was clearly mentioned on my appointment letter of the current company.

What is the problem, Rishi? my manager "Vijay Khanna" called me in his cabin and asked me to sit with the sign of his hand, pointing out his finger towards the chair.

Sir, you know I am working for this company since last eleven years and I am alone in my department, working throughout the day, no weekends, no holidays nothing. I can't take that any more so decided to move with a new assignment. I narrated everything what was inside me with an utter dare and also about the new offer I got.

See Rishi, I can understand your concerns but you know this is a very hard time we are going through. And a person like you leaving like this in such a crucial time was not expected.

Moreover, in a new organisation you need to prove yourself and your capabilities, but here we know for what you are capable for and your skills are already proved. Vijay told me in a very decent and logical manner.

We can't match your salary with the offer you got but I ensure you that after four months during April at the time of appraisals, I definitely try my best to give you some decent pay hike and also one assistant who will join you in a couple of days. You need to train him in the process to work on your behalf and get your life back. These words of Vijay put me in dilemma. This was what I wanted from the Management and leaving the job was not necessary in this case.

Within two day I got an assistant who is even more interested and energetic to know the process and his amazing go getter attitude relaxed me a lot.

It is now three months from then. After a nice weekend I came to my seat put my bag aside and opened my laptop to check the emails as usual. As soon as I opened my computer an email popped up.   That was an acknowledgement of my resignation where it was mentioned that they are relieving me with immediate effect.

Tears started flowing from my eyes, I asked myself "Is that a service reward?" or "Is that a reward of my blind trust?" A strong hand tapped by back, I turned and saw it was a office boy who came to take me to the HR department for the handover process.

It is a famous saying love your job, don't try to fall in love with your company as nobody knows when your company stop loving you. Now I can say "That is true".

Denouement: It is important to prioritize and balance professional & personal life and not let personal or personal life consume all of one's time and energy. Trusting blindly can lead to disappointment, as organisational decisions may not align with one's expectations and needs. It is also important to put continuous efforts to upgrade skills, knowledge, qualification as per the market need in order to secure future and well-being.

SELF-INTROSPECTION

Big round of applause for Anshika!! everyone was clapping around for her and the sound of clapping was somewhere hurting me. I don't know the reason but yes for me it was not a happy moment.

Hello Mr. Angad, a cute face with a decent smile broke by concentration. I took off my eyes from the 14" Laptop screen where I was working since 8:30am. Yes 8:30am, our office timing is 9:30am but I had to complete the project, so coming early as usual.

Oh Hi! I greeted. She was the new joinee in my team and her workstation was just near to mine.

So how you doing, Mr. Angad? She said this in a very polite tone stretching her eyebrows upwards and a smile on her face.

Though she had an experience of two fine years but considered as fresher in our process. All together now we were 6 team members who were working on TEAM-X-T software.

It was 5 O'clock in the evening when almost everyone was moving from office. I took my laptop and rushed towards the main door as my cab was waiting outside. Oh Sorry!! I said, as I was about the bang myself on Anshika who was coming out from the Manager's cabin with her eyes wet. It's ok! She Said.

I wanted to know what was going wrong with her and why she was upset. I put my bag down asked her about the same.

Look Angad, I had to go very urgently to meet someone today, but boss is just ruthless and wanted me to complete this assignment by today itself. I know it is urgent for the client but I had my own commitments, how can I? … she started sobbing and said "ok" I have to do, you please go, you must be getting late.

My inner conscious says how you can leave her like this Angad.

So, I decide to help her. Send me the file, I will do it and send it to you for final submission. I asked her with confidence. And please don't cry, I will help you out. You are such an amazing guy Angad but how can I give it to you, you are already late – she said while looking at me with her wet eyes. No, No Its ok please go, I will do, I said. She looked into my eyes for few seconds with a pause and said "I owe you one" and she left the office.

That day I spent next 8 hours in office till 1am to work on her presentation and put my best efforts to make it amazing.

She got the appreciation from the client for her outstanding efforts and got the promotion with a decent pay hike in just three months of her job tenure.

I tapped my back as it was my victory through her.

She came to me and said "Coffee?" may be that is the way of her gratitude. I nodded my head in yes.

From that day onwards we become friends instead of just office colleagues. I never asked about her personal life as she hadn't asked me for the same as well.

After her promotion she started working for another project but our friendship remained the same. I always helped her in making or correcting her project assignments "Just for Her" so that she can maintain her benchmarks.

That is her third promotion in a row and now she became the "Process Manager". On her "Thanks Speech" she thanked her parents, all of her previous Managers, Directors and Clients for providing unconditional support to her to achieve this corporate ladder and everyone started clapping for her.

A big question was banging on my mind that "Where am I?" do I have no relevance in her success? Or I was making myself fool working day and night to create the path for someone else who is thankless.

I was not jealous but felt ditched. When everyone was clapping then the sound of applause was hurting me like someone was scratching my wounds.

I asked myself – This is the time for self-introspection"

If you are doing something out of your capacity, working as you don't have your personal life, considering yourself available all the times, cleaning the mess spread by other colleagues and don't know how and when to say "NO' then definitely you are none other than a "People Pleaser".

It can also make you feel inauthentic, because when you are smiling on the outside–despite feeling frustrated from inside–you are essentially pretending to be someone who you are not. In fact, smiling to appease others when you are not genuinely feeling happy is linked to a decreased sense of well-being.

And certainly, this is the time for "**Self-Introspection**".

Denouement: It is important to prioritize self-care and be mindful of how much you are sacrificing for others. Being a "people pleaser" by constantly doing more than what is expected from you and not setting boundaries can lead to negative feelings and decreased well-being. It is crucial to take a step back and reflect on your own needs and emotions in order to maintain a healthy balance in your personal and professional life.

                    Author: Pankaj Chandan

BLESSING IN DISGUISE

Anxiety and nervousness were clearly banging on the face of Sanjeev while getting ready for an interview with top rated Multinational Company "Aayan Enterprises Limited" in Okhla, New Delhi and today is the show day.

Sanjeev who was in his early 30's was living in a rented apartment in Faridabad, far away for the sake of job from his parents who were living in a remote area of Punjab.

He started his carrier when he was just 22 years old. With lot of hard-work and determination over 8 years of his professional journey he reached to the level of Manager – Human Resource.

After approx. 45 minutes of his travel, he finally reached in front of the multi-story building where he supposed to come for an interview.

He reached 15 minutes before the scheduled interview timing. Sitting in reception he was just memorising latest updates, laws, strategies and brushing up his knowledge of HR field as every candidate do before appearing for an interview.

"Hello Mr. Sanjeev" – a loud but mesmerising voice of a receptionist from a very silent reception area broke his concentration who escorted him to the meeting room where the panel was waiting for him.

After a long discussion of more than two hours, he finally left from there positively.

Everybody liked his candidature, promising attitude and impressed with his efforts towards his current job carrier.

Aayan Enterprises Limited was very new in telecom operations and wanted to establish very good and dedicated team within very short span of time and energy considering the very less time to start the overseas operations. As Sanjeev is also working in telecom-based organisation and was the key person to start the company from scratch to nearly 350 employees in a row, so his chances were bright for the selection.

Likewise, he called up for two more rounds of interview on different dates. He got the confirmation that he is the only one who cleared all the rounds and finally CEO wanted to meet him and on the same day they will give him the letter of offer.

On forth but final round of interview with CEO who appeared to be very friendly and calm just opposite of the expectation of Sanjeev who had the different image of the CEO Position in his mind. It was an amazing round of interview.

They had discussed the future planning of the upcoming project, manpower, Incentives and other areas of concerns.

It was more than half an hour Sanjeev was sitting in reception and was waiting for his offer letter.

Will you please check as I am waiting for my offer letter? Sanjeev said this in a very polite tone to the receptionist. She nodded her head, asked him to sit, and started dialling intercom number. After a little discussion, she hung up the phone.

Mr. Sanjeev, you can go HR Department will be in touch with you, receptionist said with a smile.

Although two weeks have passed since he applied for a job at Aayan Enterprises, he has yet to receive a call or any response from them.

Months passed, Sanjeev noticed a change in the attendance of the staff, where previously punctual employees were now taking more leaves than usual.

The sudden resignation of several key personnel from the company on such a short notice sent shockwaves to the entire organization. The organisation was facing the daunting task of replacing key personnel in such a short notice. This created a sense of uncertainty and insecurity among the remaining staff.

One day the Vipin who was working as an executive HR came to Sanjeev and said "Sir, I wanted to tell you something". Yes, Vipin tell me what is the matter? Sanjeev said. Actually Sir, I got selected for an Assistant Manager Position, Vipin said this with a shining smile and continued – and I have to join in 10 days of time.

I know policy bounds me for 1 months' notice but please help me to get early relieving. During the conversation unknowingly Vipin reveals that he got the offer from Aayan Enterprises.

Listening to that Sanjeev got a sudden shock when he came to know that most of the employees had got the calls even they had not applied there. It was a clear sign of "Pouching".

Sanjeev got the sense of utter unprofessionalism of Aayan' Enterprises, before they could damage more, Sanjeev and his company's management quickly sprang into action, putting together a recruitment plan to find suitable replacements for the departed personnel. A thorough selection process was implemented to ensure that the new hires would be able to perform the roles to the same level as the former employees.

At the same time, Sanjeev stated one to one training sessions to create a sense of security among the staff.

He implemented more attractive incentive and reward system to ensure that the remaining staff were recognized for their efforts. They also organized regular team building activities and relaxed the work environment to encourage a sense of camaraderie.

The transition period was relatively smooth and the company was soon back on track. The staff morale has also improved significantly, as the employees felt more secure and appreciated.

It had been four years since then. One fine morning at 7:00 am, Sanjeev was enjoying his cup of tea on his balcony chair with his newspaper. As he was an avid reader and always kept himself updated on the latest news and events. On this particular morning, he was scanning through the headlines, one caught his attention. The headline read, "Aayan Enterprises Limited" is in the prosses of shut down due to heavy operational losses and employees are on strike as they were not paid since last 6 months.

He quickly read the article and learned that the company had been accused of exploiting its employees, long working hours and even not following labour laws.

"Blessing in disguise" Sanjeev said to himself, putting his newspaper down and looking towards the sky thinking of that day when he appeared for an interview there, a lavish office, big fat salaries but no principles, fairness and professionalism. Thank God I am not a part of this.

Denouement: Maintaining professionalism and ethical conduct in the workplace / industry is paramount to achieving long-term success and stability for any organization. Unprofessional behaviour, on the other hand, can create an environment of instability and decreased staff morale.

Moreover, ethical considerations must be a priority in all business decisions, as they can impact not only the bottom line but also the reputation of the company. This means upholding values such as honesty, transparency, and fairness, and avoiding any actions that could be perceived as unethical or fraudulent.

By prioritizing professionalism and ethics in the workplace / industry, a company can create a culture of trust and respect, which can lead to increased employee satisfaction, productivity, and ultimately, business success.

RACE OF EFFORTS

Shama was a recruiter with a large corporation, and she was known for her excellent track record of finding top talent for the company. She had been with the company for several years and had developed a good reputation among her colleagues and superiors.

One day, Shama took a much-needed vacation to recharge and relax. She had been working hard for months, and she was looking forward to spend some time away from the office with the family.

Unfortunately, while she was on leave, her colleague Manpreet took advantage of her absence and stole her diary from her cupboard where she had written all the important contact numbers and future leads.

Manpreet was astonished to saw her diary and her way ahead future planning of hiring candidates along with the contact numbers. She got greedy and wanted to encash an opportunity to make some extra incentive by contacting the future candidates of Shama.

Shama was not aware what had happened in her absence.

After her joining, one day she saw some of the candidate arrived for the interview and that were the same she already shortlisted and kept them on hold for future hiring. She shocked and angry when she discovered that they were with the reference of Manpreet.

Manpreet, how you know the candidates came today for an interview? Said Shama while confronting her. No.. No.. I know them and they were already in touch with me since long. She replied in a fumbling tone.

Manpreet, however, was not remorseful and instead tried to defend her actions. She claimed that he had done nothing wrong, and that she was only trying to help the company by finding more qualified candidates.

Shama was devastated by Manpreet's betrayal, and she reported the incident to her superiors after thorough investigation. But nothing had happened and no action was taken against her. Even Shama was blamed to be rude to her and bring her down.

"One more experience counted", Shama smiled and asked herself.

Despite the setback, she continued to excel in her job and was eventually promoted to a higher position within the company. She learned to trust her instincts and to always be on the lookout for people who might try to take advantage of her.

People can come into your life and try to bring you down, telling you that you're not good enough or that you won't succeed. It's important to recognize these negative influences and stand up for yourself. Don't let anyone demotivate you, instead, focus on what makes you unique and use that to propel yourself forward. There will always be people who try to ditch you, but don't let them define your life. Believe in yourself and prove to everyone that you are the best.

Denouement: In order to navigate the complexities of professional life, it is essential to cultivate a strong sense of self-awareness and trust in one's own instincts. It is equally important to recognize and avoid negative influences that may hinder progress, and to maintain a steadfast commitment to personal and professional growth.

To achieve success, it is crucial to resist the influence of external forces and avoid being defined by the opinions of others. This requires a strong sense of self-assurance and a willingness to stand up for oneself in the face of setbacks and betrayals.

In short, cultivating self-awareness, trusting one's instincts, and maintaining a resilient mindset are all essential components of achieving success in a professional context. By prioritizing these values, individuals can rise above adversity and thrive in their chosen field.

<u>TAKE A STAND</u>

Ritika had been working in a small factory for the past few years.

She was a single mother so had lot of responsibilities towards her family and child.

She was the only female employee and the only one who faced frequent sexual harassment from her male co-workers.

Anuj who was her colleague in the same process had some bad intentions and always passing comments in the double meaning words.

At first, it was just occasional comments and glances that made her uncomfortable but soon it escalated to more serious forms of harassment when he started gossiping around with other male colleagues while looking at her.

She was constantly touched inappropriately and faced lewd comments on a daily basis. Ritika tried her best to ignore Anuj's inappropriate behaviour, but it was becoming increasingly difficult.

She was scared to speak up as no one would believe and all of them would gang up against her.

Knowing that she was in a vulnerable position and that her complaints would likely be ignored by the authorities. One day, Anuj had crossed the line.

Madam Ji aaj to pataka lag rahi ho! Anuj said while looking her from top to bottom in a very vulgar way.

During late evening when everyone was leaving the factory premises Anuj approached her in the factory in some isolated place and tried to force himself on her. Ritika was terrified and managed to fight him off, but not before suffering some physical injuries.

The incident shook Ritika to her core and she was determined to "Take A Stand" no matter what. She reported the incident to her supervisor and narrated everything, who took the matter seriously and launched an internal investigation.

Anuj tried to manipulate the entire scenario and started blaming her and her character though the help of his other male colleague friends in the factory and also pressurised her to take the compliant back.

Ritika had decided not to step back for any reason.

After a thorough review and exploring the evidences, the investigation concluded that the

Anuj was indeed guilty of sexual harassment and was terminated from the company with immediate effect.

Ritika was relieved that the matter had been resolved and that the perpetrators had been punished. However, the incident had taken a toll on her mental and emotional health. She was scarred by the experience and it took her a long time to come to terms with what had happened.

She eventually decided to move on and continue working at the factory. She had learnt an important lesson: that it was important to speak up when faced with sexual harassment.

Ritika's story is an important reminder of the fact that no one should ever have to experience sexual harassment in the workplace irrespective of the gender determination. It should be taken seriously and dealt with accordingly.

There is no excuse for sexual harassment and it should never be encouraged. Those who commit sexual harassment should be held accountable for their actions and face the consequences.

Harassment in the workplace is often unreported due to social concerns (log kya kahegae). Fear of charges will not be believed or taken seriously. Worry about losing job and moreover, economic impact on their family or those who rely on them.

Denouement: In any workplace, it is crucial that individuals are able to feel safe and respected. Unfortunately, sexual harassment is an all-too-common occurrence that can severely impact victims and the overall work environment. In these situations, it is crucial that victims speak up and take a stand, despite the challenges and obstacles they may face.

Perpetrators of sexual harassment must be held accountable for their actions, and it is imperative that victims report any incidents to appropriate authorities. Fear and social concerns should not prevent victims from seeking justice and taking necessary action to ensure their safety.

Moreover, it is important to recognize that sexual harassment is not acceptable in any circumstance, and everyone has the right to a safe and respectful work environment, regardless of gender. It is the responsibility of all employees to actively prevent and address any behaviours that are not in line with this fundamental right.

By creating a culture that prioritizes safety and respect for all individuals, we should work towards eradicating sexual harassment in the workplace and ensuring that all employees can work in an environment that is free from such harmful behaviours.

POWER PARADOX

ISG India was a large corporation that had been in business for many years. The company had always been successful, but recently, the business had been struggling to stay competitive even though investing lot of money into business with very experienced manpower available.

The board of directors was faced with the challenge of turning the company around, but they were unable to reach a consensus on the most effective course of action. While some directors advocated for cost-cutting measures, others were in favour of investing in new technology and marketing campaigns. However, the root cause of the company's sudden downturn was not being discussed, indicating that there was an important piece missing from the overall picture.

The board was at an impasse, and the CEO of the company was becoming increasingly frustrated. He knew that something had to be done, but he wasn't sure what.

One day, the CEO decided to bring in a consultant to help him find a solution. The consultant suggested that the board and the CEO look at the role of corporate politics in their decision-making process.

The consultant explained that corporate politics can often influence strategic decisions in ways that are not always obvious. He said that power dynamics within the organization can have a huge impact on how decisions are made, and the board needed to be aware of this.

The consultant suggested that the board create a committee to investigate the role of corporate politics in their decision-making. The committee would be tasked with evaluating the power dynamics within the organization and how they were influencing decisions.

The board agreed to the consultant's suggestion and created the committee. After a few months of investigating, the committee concluded that corporate politics were indeed playing a large role in the company's decision-making process.

The board then implemented a number of changes to the way decisions were made. They created a system of checks and balances to ensure that decisions were based on the best interests of the company, rather than on the agendas of individual board members.

The company went on to become more successful and profitable than ever before. The CEO and the board of directors realized that it was important to be aware of the role of corporate politics in their decision-making process and to adjust their strategy accordingly.

Politics on be in power position can have a significant impact on strategic decisions and it is important for organizations to be aware of this. By understanding and managing the power dynamics within the organization, leaders can ensure that their decisions are based on the best interests of the company, rather than on the agendas of themselves.

There are many reasons why people want power in an organisation. Some of the reasons people seek power in an organisation are to gain control and influence over decision-making, to advance their personal agendas or career aspirations, or to make a positive difference in the organisation.

On the positive side, having empowered people in an organisation can lead to better decision-making, increased efficiency, and better morale. When individuals are given the power to make decisions, they are likely to take ownership of their roles and be more motivated to contribute to the organisation's success. A strong leader with the ability to delegate can create an environment in which everyone feels empowered to contribute their ideas and opinions.

On the negative side, having too much power in the hands of one individual can be detrimental to the organisation. It can lead to a lack of accountability and transparency, creating a culture of fear and intimidation. It can also result in favouritism and nepotism, and can prevent the free flow of ideas and creativity. Too much power in one person's hands can also lead to a lack of diversity in decision-making, and can reduce the effectiveness of the organisation.

In Denouement, having empowered individuals in an organisation can be beneficial if used in the right way. However, it is important to ensure that power is distributed fairly and that it is not concentrated in one person's hands. This will ensure that everyone in the organisation is able to contribute and that decisions are made in an equitable and transparent manner.

Critical job position and attitude of the key persons who are holding that position in the organisation and influencing decisions of the top management

The critical job positions in any organization are pivotal to the success of an organization, as they require an individual with strong leadership skills and a deep understanding of the company's goals and objectives. However, when an individual in a critical job position engages in office politics or attempts to influence decisions of the top management, it can be detrimental to the organization's success.

In the modern business environment, it is not uncommon for employees to engage in office politics in order to gain favour with higher-ups and increase their chances of success. While this can be beneficial in some cases, it can also have negative consequences. Employees who attempt to influence decisions of the top management may do so for their own personal gain, rather than for the benefit of the organization. This can lead to a breakdown in communication between the top management and the employees, as well as a lack of trust between the two parties. As a result, decision-making can become inefficient and the organization's performance can suffer.

Furthermore, an individual in a critical job position who is engaging in office politics may be putting their own career ahead of the organization's interests. This can create a hostile work environment and discourage other employees from speaking up and taking initiative. This can lead to a lack of innovation and creativity, as employees may be afraid to voice their ideas out of fear of being wrongly judged or punished.

It is important for organizations to recognize the role that critical job positions play in their success and to ensure that employees in these positions are held to the highest standards. Employees in critical job positions should be focused on the organization's goals and objectives and should not be engaging in office politics or attempting to influence decisions of the top management. Doing so can have a negative impact on the organization's performance and can prevent the organization from reaching its full potential.

FROM ROOKIES TO ROCKSTARS

Welcome to the corporate world rookies!

The corporate world can be a great place to work, build relationships and advance your career. But like all environments, it can also be a place of politics and power struggles. As a new joiner, it is important to be aware of the potential pitfalls and to take steps to ensure that you don't get trapped in corporate politics.

First, it is important to focus on your work and your performance. While networking and building relationships with colleagues is important, make sure that you don't lose sight of what you were hired to do. Doing your job well is the best way to avoid getting caught up in corporate politics.

Second, be aware of what is going on around you. Although it is important to focus on your work, it is also important to be aware of the power dynamics in the office. Pay attention to who is being promoted and who is being side-lined. Notice who has influence in the company and who seems to be having a hard time.

Third, try to stay neutral. Corporate politics can get ugly, and it is important to try to stay out of it. Don't take sides or get involved in disputes. Don't gossip or spread rumours. And don't be tempted to get involved in power struggles or backstabbing.

Finally, don't be afraid to speak up. If you see something that isn't right, don't be afraid to speak up and say something. It can be difficult to do this, but it is important to stand up for what is right. You don't have to get involved in the politics, but you can still make your voice heard.

The corporate world can be a great place to work, but it is important to be aware of the potential pitfalls and to take steps to ensure that you don't get trapped in corporate politics. By focusing on your work, staying neutral and speaking up when necessary, you can avoid the worst of the politics and make sure that your experience in the corporate world is a positive one.

INSIDER SECRETS:

UNLOCKING

THE VAULT OF SUCCESS

1. Always stay ahead of the game by staying informed and up-to-date on the latest developments within your organization.

2. Never forget to take time to build relationships with your colleagues, as these relationships can be invaluable when navigating the corporate landscape.

3. Don't be afraid to voice your opinion, as long as it is backed up by facts and sound reasoning.

4. Always treat your colleagues with respect.

5. Take time to understand the politics of the organization and the people who are influencing decisions.

6. Don't be afraid to ask questions when you don't understand something.

7. If you don't understand something, don't be afraid to ask for clarification.

8. Always remain professional, even when dealing with difficult situations.

9. Be flexible and open to different perspectives.

10. Network with others in your organization and beyond to gain insights into different areas of the business.

11. Know when to speak up or stay quiet.

12. Always be honest and transparent.

13. Make sure to keep track of the different lines of communication in the organization.

14. Be willing to take risks if you believe in the outcome.

15. Don't be afraid to disagree, but do it respectfully.

16. Listen to understand, not to reply.

17. Respect the chain of command and follow the rules.

18. Take responsibility for your actions and their consequences.

19. Don't gossip or spread rumours.

20. Always focus on the bigger picture.

Author: Pankaj Chandan